WHAT I EAT

Written By
E.C. Andrews

Letters from Around the World

KidHaven PUBLISHING

Published in 2025 by
KidHaven Publishing, an Imprint of
Greenhaven Publishing, LLC
2544 Clinton St., Buffalo, NY 14224

Written by: E.C. Andrews
Edited by: Elise Carraway
Designed by: Amelia Harris

Cataloging-in-Publication Data

Names: Andrews, E.C.
Title: What I eat / E.C. Andrews.
Description: Buffalo, New York : KidHaven Publishing, 2025. | Series: Letters from around the world | Includes glossary and index.
Identifiers: ISBN 9781534546868 (pbk.) | ISBN 9781534546875 (library bound) | ISBN 9781534546882 (ebook)
Subjects: LCSH: Food--Juvenile literature. | Food habits--Juvenile literature.
Classification: LCC TX355.A534 2025 | DDC 394.1'2--dc23

Manufactured in the United States of America

CPSIA compliance information: Batch #CSKH25
For further information contact Greenhaven Publishing LLC at 1-844-317-7404.

Image Credits

All images are courtesy of Shutterstock.com, unless otherwise specified. With thanks to Getty Images, Thinkstock Photo, and iStockphoto.

Cover images – NataLT, Akane1988, estherpoon, Fourleaflover, Puwadol Jaturawutthichai, Tartila, The img, Colorfuel Studio, Jeppe Gustafsson, Ground Picture. Recurring images – KanKhem, Olga_C. 2 – ina9, inspiring.team. 4–5 – Charles Brutlag, Robert J. Bradshaw, WinWin artlab. 6–7 – Bibadash, HikoPhotography, grafvision, designers circle. 8–9 – Vijayography, StockImageFactory.com, TwoStock, Navakun Suwantragul, matsukiyo8379, Arunagren. 10–11 – Ketmut, Dudaeva, JM Travel Photography, nblx, Alen Ka, Illerlok_xolms, StockBURIN. 12–13 – summer studio, SMarina, Kert, Karen Culp, WinWin artlab. 14–15 – Geshas, Chatham172, Fanfo, inspiring.team, Vector Tradition. 16–17 – Raffaella Galvani, Gaus Alex, from my point of view, inspiring.team. 18–19 – CatherineScarlett, Natalia Lisovskaya, Osacr_Y, Ricky Aditya Perdana, inspiring.team. 20–21 – Aninka Bongers-Sutherland, Natken, Thao Lan, WinWin artlab. 22–23 – AnnaStills, Mario Magido, Hein Nouwens.

CONTENTS

Words that look like this can be found in the glossary on page 24.

LETTERS FROM EVERYWHERE

Hello! My name is James. I live in the U.S. I love cooking. I write letters to my pen pals from around the world to ask what their favorite thing to eat is.

My favorite food is biscuits and gravy. Our traditional American biscuits are light and fluffy. Our gravy is a white sauce. My family like to make ours using bacon fat. Biscuits in the United States are savory.

American biscuits and gravy

A LETTER FROM JAPAN

Hi! I am Kaito. I live in Japan. Here, we have lots of different kinds of noodles. On cold days, my parents make noodles with hot broth, eggs, and vegetables. This is called ramen noodle soup.

We also eat a lot of rice and seafood. One of my favorite dishes is sushi. Sushi is traditionally made with rice, fish, and vegetables. It is often wrapped in seaweed and is eaten with chopsticks.

It can take 10 years to become a sushi chef!

A LETTER FROM INDIA

Hello. I am Diya. I am from India. When walking home from school, I like to buy a snack called vada pav. Vada pav is made of spicy mashed potatoes that are deep-fried in chickpea batter.

Vada pav is served in a bread bun.

In the evening, I help my family make dinner. We often have curry. My favorite curry is saag. We make saag with spinach and mustard greens. We eat it with rice and roti.

A LETTER FROM ITALY

Hello. I am Lorenzo. I live in Italy. Italy is the home of pizza. Pizza has been around for a very long time. I like my pizza with prosciutto, which is a type of Italian ham.

For dessert, we often have gelato. Gelato might seem similar to ice cream but is actually quite different. It has a much stronger flavor than ice cream. My favorite gelato flavors are vanilla and strawberry.

Summer can be very warm in Italy. Gelato is the perfect treat!

A LETTER FROM MEXICO

Hi. I am Sofia from Mexico. My friends and I love to make tacos. Tacos are made with curved tortillas. You can put whatever fillings you like in them. You eat tacos with your hands.

I like my tacos with black beans and guacamole.

Afterwards, we like to have churros. Churros are like stick-shaped doughnuts. After they are fried, they are dusted with cinnamon and sugar. My friends and I dip ours in warm chocolate sauce!

We make churros at home as a special treat.

A LETTER FROM TÜRKIYE

Hello. I am Emine. I live in Türkiye. My favorite meal is called imam bayildi. The name means "the imam fainted." Some say it is named after an imam who fainted because it was so delicious!

Imam bayildi is a roasted eggplant that is stuffed with garlic, onions, and tomatoes. Traditionally, it is made with only vegetables and no meat. I like to have mine with a cup of spiced tea.

A LETTER FROM FRANCE

Hi there. I am Louis. I am from France. As a treat, my family and I like to make cheese soufflés. A soufflé rises when it is baked, making it very fluffy and warm.

A soufflé is very tricky to make.

On a more casual day, my family and I sometimes make ratatouille. Ratatouille is a type of stew made with chopped eggplant, tomatoes, and zucchini. It is simple to make and very healthy.

And delicious!

A LETTER FROM CHINA

Hi. I am Mei. I am from China. Before I go to school, I often eat xiao long bao. Xiao long bao are a kind of Chinese dumpling. You can have them with meat or vegetables.

Xiao long bao are often cooked in bamboo baskets.

My favorite food is a traditional dish called Peking duck. Peking duck is a dish made with slices of slow-roasted, crispy duck. The duck is rolled up in thin pancakes.

Peking duck is served with green onions and sauce.

A LETTER FROM SOUTH AFRICA

Hey there. My name is Banele. I am from South Africa. One of my favorite things to eat is called chakalaka. It is made with beans, tomatoes, garlic, and cabbage mixed into a curry paste.

I eat chakalaka with mealie, or corn, bread.

Mealie bread

Do you like dessert? There is a traditional South African dessert called a melktert that I love! Melktert means "milk tart." It has a sweet pastry crust with a smooth, sweet filling of milk, flour, sugar, and eggs.

Many South African families have their own melktert recipes.

EVERYWHERE IS DIFFERENT

The food people eat is different in every country. I love reading all my pen pals' letters about the traditional recipes they get to enjoy. I hope I can try some of them one day.

Which food would you like to try? Are there any types of foods that are unique to your country? Why not write me a letter about it? I would love to read about some more amazing foods!

GLOSSARY

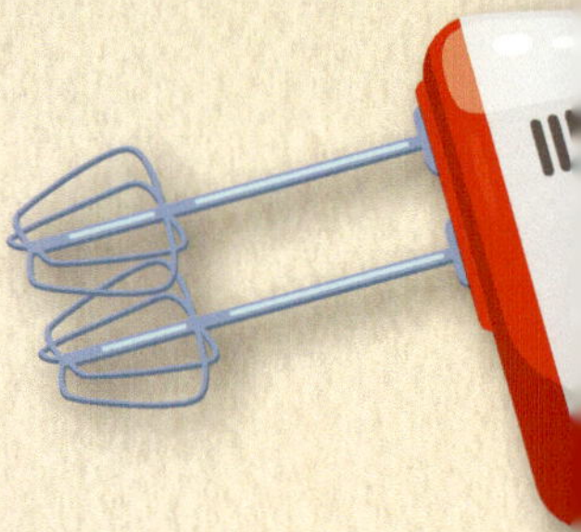

broth	a soup that is made with the liquid from meat or vegetables
chopsticks	a pair of thin sticks used for eating food
deep-fried	when something is cooked by being dipped into boiling oil
imam	a person who leads prayers at a Muslim mosque
pastry	a flat dough often used as a base for pies and tarts
recipes	instructions on how to cook certain dishes
savory	having a salty or spicy flavor
tortillas	thin flatbreads that are made to be eaten with a filling
traditional	to do with something that has been done for a long time
unique	unlike anything or anyone else

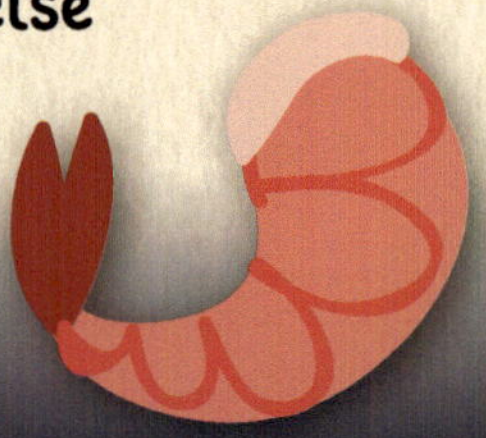

INDEX